To those who have supported my music and song "How Would You Like To Be Me", much love. I dedicate this book to anyone who has been through any type of racism or discrimination. Stay strong and remain proud of who you are, always. To the generations of people to come, I hope this book can play an education role in influencing positive change for a better future where you are all treated with fairness, kindness, equality, dignity, love and respect regardless of race or colour.

Special thanks to Agnieszka Pastorok-Korzeniowska, you did an amazing job making my vision come to life with the illustrations. You are such a talented artist, it's been a great honour to have you apart of this creation.

Special thanks to Amy Corbett for the proofread, much appreciated.

I acknowledge the Traditional Owners throughout Australia and pay my respects to Elders past, present and emerging.

HOW WOULD YOU LIKE TO BE ME

Written by Colin Darcy AKA Caper
Illustrated by Agnieszka Pastorok-Korzeniowska

How Would You Like to Be Me – Unpacking everyday Racism

As you begin this journey, I ask that you carry yourself with integrity and approach these pages with respect.

You're now about to experience illustrations that show what racism and casual racism is alongside Caper's lyrics of his popular song "How Would You Like To Be Me". It's time to unpack their meaning. These words invite you to pause and step into another perspective. This isn't just about reading or listening, this is where the real work begins.

Take a moment before answering each question, reflect deeply and honestly and use the questions to spark important, sometimes uncomfortable, conversations. Challenge what you've been taught and think critically about racism and casual racism, not as a distant issue, but as something that is present right now in systems, language, and everyday life.

Let's Go!

From Verse 1: How Would You Like To Be Me? / An Aborigine / Looked down upon in society...

Discussion Prompt:

- After seeing the impact of racism on Caper, imagine if that were your everyday reality, how do you think it would make you feel?

- What do you think it would feel like to be judged negatively before someone even knows you, just because of your identity?

- Where do people learn racist attitudes and behaviours, and how can we unlearn them?

- How might being stereotyped and treated unfairly from childhood into adulthood affect someone's confidence, self-esteem, and identity?

From Verse 1: By ignorant little suckers that make you feel odd / Think that all we do is drink grog...

Discussion Prompts:

- What are some common stereotypes you've heard about Aboriginal people?

- Where do these ideas come from, and why are they so harmful?

- If people constantly judged you based on these stereotypes, how might it affect how you see yourself

- Why do harmful stereotypes about Aboriginal people still exist today?

From Verse 1: Was just at a pizza bar the other day... Overheard a conversation and I heard em say, "Black Boongs this... And Black Niggers that..." Made me wanna react and say something back.

Discussion Prompts:

- Imagine you were Caper in that moment in the pizza bar, what would it feel like to overhear those words about you or your culture?

- What can we do or say to interrupt racism without resorting to violence?

- How would you feel being exposed to that kind of language regularly?

From Chorus 1: How Would You Like To Be Me? / Stereotype? / What should I paint myself white, to fit in right?...

Reflection Prompts:

- Why do people sometimes feel pressure to change who they are in order to be accepted?

- Have you ever felt left out or judged for being different? How did it affect you?

From Verse 2: Taxi man says the night's been busy / Then goes on to say he hates picking up "Abos"...

Discussion Prompts:

- Why is the word "Abo" considered offensive and hurtful?

- Imagine your Caper in the taxi, if someone said something racist not knowing you were Aboriginal, how would that make you feel?

- Why is it important to speak up when you hear offensive language?

- What are respectful ways you can challenge racism in your community?

CAN YOU BELIEVE THE NERVE, I SAID DON'T YOU KNOW THAT'S A RACIST WORD?

From Verse 2: Ya quick to help others in need, every time there's another tsunami / What about in our own country?... What about Aboriginal communities?

Critical Thinking Prompts:

- Why do some Aboriginal communities still face poverty and limited opportunities?

- What do you understand about colonisation and its ongoing impacts today?

- How would you feel growing up in a community that is often overlooked or underfunded?

- What does fairness look like when we talk about Closing the Gap, Reconciliation, and Self-Determination? (If you don't know those terms, please research what they are and then answer)

- Why do you think Australia voted no to a "Voice to Parliament" in 2023?

- Do you think a "Voice to Parliament" would have helped to fix challenging issues in Aboriginal communities?

From Verse 3: To the media, don't stereotype us every time / Gang 49 does a crime... Cause the public look at us like we all bad, and it's makin us mad.

Media Literacy Prompts:

- How does media shape the way people think about different cultural groups?

- Do you often see positive news stories about Aboriginal people in mainstream or social media? If not, why do you think that is?

- Can you think of a time when an Aboriginal person was treated unfairly/portrayed negatively in the news or on social media? What impact do you think that had on them and the wider community? If you can't think of one, Adam Goodes racial slur story is a good example. Please feel free to google it for more information.

- If you were constantly portrayed negatively in the media, how do you think it would affect your self-worth?

From Verse 3: Lining up at a club... the bouncer said sorry, but I can't let you in, cause the colour of ya skin...

Discussion Prompts:

- Imagine you're Caper lining up at the club and the bouncer said that to you, what do you think it would feel like to be denied access to something because of your skin colour?

- How would you want your friends or community to support you in that moment?

- Have you ever witnessed or experienced discrimination? What did it feel like?

- If you witnessed something like this and there was a support line available, would you report it? If not, why?

Final Chorus: "Discriminated? Hated? / And judged by society? / Tell me, how would you like to be me?"

Final Reflection:

- Imagine yourself in each of the situations Caper described. How might that shape your everyday life?

- How would it feel to be hated or judged simply because of your heritage and skin colour?

- How can we support those around us who feel excluded, stereotyped, discriminated, racially profiled, teased or judged?

- What actions can we take to build empathy, fairness, and challenge racism in our communities, workplaces and schools?

- Do you think there should be policy changes in Australia (such as updates to the racial discrimination act) to better recognise and enforce that engaging in racism is illegal? If no, why? If yes, how can we achieve this? i.e. through greater consequences such as fines or jail time.

- Will you choose to stay silent, or will you speak up and call it out when you witness racism happening?

How Would You Like To Be Me (Full Song Lyrics)

Verse 1

How Would You Like To Be Me?
An Aborigine
Looked down upon in society

How would like to be treated like a dog?
By ignorant little suckers that make u feel odd
Think that all we do is drink grog

And they say we only have ourselves to blame
Those idiots should be ashamed
It's like they can't and won't understand Aboriginal pain

I wish those haters can walk in our shoes
Then they'll know what it's like to lose
And live a life that's been abused

From hereditary ills
That kill

Hey!! Was just at a pizza bar the other day
Overheard a conversation and I heard em say
Black Boongs this... And Black Niggers that

Made me wanna react
And say something back

With my fists
Cause I was pissed!!!

But I didn't wild out and act a fool
Cause violence don't change a thing at all
Don't change at thing at all...

Chorus

How Would You Like To Be Me?
Stereotype?
What should I paint myself white?
To fit in right?

How Would You Like To Be Me?
Discriminated? Hated?
And judged by society?

Tell me How Would You Like To Be Me?...

Verse 2

In a taxi on the way to the city
Taxi man says the nights been busy

Then goes onto say he hates picking up Abo's
I was like what the hell, Abo's?
Can u believe the nerve!
I said don't you know that's a racist word?

He said oh... I didn't realise you were black
I said even if I wasn't you shouldn't say that

Now how would you like to be me?
Treated like a freggin disease
Or surrounded by poverty?

Ya quick to help others in need
Every time there's another tsunami

What about in our own country?
What about Aboriginal communities?

They too live in third world conditions food and fuel cost more
Hey, housing and people in it are poor

Health is the biggest killer, but hey people don't care
As long as the Blacks stay there
Now that's unfair...

Chorus

How Would You Like To Be Me?
Stereotype?
What should I paint myself white?
To fit in right?

How Would You Like To Be Me?
Discriminated? Hated?

And judged by society?

Tell me How Would You Like To Be Me?...

Verse 3

To the media don't stereotype us every time
Gang 49 does a crime

Cause the public look at us like we all bad
And it's makin us mad

Now how would you like to be me?
Lining up at a club
Wasn't drunk

Dressed fresh to death
Bouncer put my patience to the test

Spent an hour in the line
Got to the front was like about damn time

Then the bouncer said sorry, but I can't let you in
A fight broke out last night between Blacks and an Asian

I was like that wasn't me I wasn't him
He said I can't let you in
Because the colour of ya skin

Now that took the cake
Cause the bouncer was African American for peace sake!

Know what I'm saying?...

Chorus

How Would You Like To Be Me?
Stereotype?
What should I paint myself white?
To fit in right?

How Would You Like To Be Me?
Discriminated? Hated?
And judged by society?

Tell me How Would You Like To Be Me?...

Closing words from Colin Darcy:

Writing "How Would You Like To Be Me" was like therapy for me, I wrote the song the day after the pizza bar incident. By this point I had had enough and needed to express my anger, pain and frustration that had been building up inside since a kid. The irony was when the video for the song was released online, it got banned on Facebook because someone found the lyrical content offensive or triggering. The video ban made national, and then international headlines, which brought the issue of racism to the forefront. It gained a lot of positive support, but also more racism, you can see the racist comments clearly in the video comment section on YouTube. This was also my first experience of people who were white sending me threats via social media. I remember at that time questioning how people can be so cruel and evil, sitting cowardly behind a screen, sending horrible things that affected both myself and my girlfriend at the time. But, I guess we've seen throughout history how the world has always been like that, once Black people are projected on larger platforms or are speaking up for Black people's rights, they become moving targets and are even shot down, such as Dr Martin Luther King Jnr and Malcom X. Adam Goodes is a perfect example here in Australia, a man who was a victim of a racist slur, called out this racism on the footy field, and in return was portrayed by the media and many in the public eye as the enemy. This incident led to him getting booed each time he went near a footy on the field, a bullying tactic by the crowd, which in in my eyes led Adam to an early retirement.

I recently saw Stan Grant speak during his 2025 Reconciliation Lecture in Melbourne, he spoke a little bit about his decision to step down from the TV show Q&A. I advise you all to research who Stan Grant is. To me, Stan sounded like someone who had been through a lot, he spoke about the threats he had received from people and how that affected him and his family deeply. We should never have to feel this way, especially when we take on the burden of trying to unpack racism and call out past and current wrongs. We shouldn't be threatened with violence when we stand up and fight for what's right. We shouldn't have to bury the truth. But, I guess many people don't like hearing the truth, because it forces them to reflect, to look in the mirror, and confront who they really are. And for some, that's deeply uncomfortable. It's easier to stay in ignorance, because for them, ignorance is bliss.

When "How Would You Like To Be Me" was released, I pitched it to Triple J, which many in Australia know is a popular radio station which at the time played less commercial music. One of the hosts got back to me and said they wouldn't play it, said it wasn't strong enough. I still wonder to this day whether it was due to the lyrical content, the country wasn't ready for it. Because the song is raw truth-telling in its purest form. When I was accepted in 2013 to perform live on national TV on the Marngrook Footy Show, the show director told me I couldn't perform "How Would You Like To Be Me" because they were afraid it would make their white audience uncomfortable. Then again, in 2018, when I performed at the Adelaide 36ers MVP night, I was told not to perform the same song. It's no coincidence. They were scared of the same thing, that I'd make their white audience uncomfortable. But in 2015, when I opened for Nelly in Adelaide in front of 5,000 people, I saw people in the front row singing every word. And in 2017, when I performed at the Port Adelaide Football Club, Aboriginal kids were singing my song word for word. Ironically 8 years later, it featured in a movie on Netflix titled "A Second Chance Rivals". This was one of the proudest moments of my life, to hear my song being played in the rolling credits of a movie at a cinema. As well as that, a grade 10 English teacher in Portugal asked for my permission to use my lyrics as part of a learning book to teach her students about racism, which of course I agreed to. That was 14 years ago, which now has led me to creating my own educational resource. I also reflect to this day, it's crazy how people in another country can embrace, see value, show love and support, and proactively use my art to influence change, whereas my home country has not done this.

The impact of racism on me has been profound, not just emotionally, but physically. It's something I've faced since I was a kid and has caused ongoing stress, anxiety, and depression. It has even manifested in my body through chronic inflammation. These experiences have played a significant role in my ongoing struggle with PTSD. It has taken years to learn how to consciously regulate my nervous system in response to the fight or flight reactions triggered by racism, and even now, it remains a daily practice.

A small but telling example, I still feel anxious every time I line up at a cafe to order a coffee. I often have to consciously slow my breathing and remind myself that I'm safe, that I'm not in danger. This response traces back to the traumatic experience I had when I was denied entry into a nightclub. Not long after, police arrived. When I tried to explain what had happened, one officer pushed me aggressively and threatened to arrest me if I didn't keep quiet. That same Adelaide club was later sued by an Aboriginal woman who experienced the exact same discrimination, and she won. Justice in that case was served. But these incidents are not rare, they are ongoing. I speak more about these lived realities in my song "Unbelievable", released under my new artist name, Col Darcy.

My hope is that this book helps others truly understand what racism is, not just in theory, but in the real and painful ways it affects people like me. Racism can be deeply traumatic and stressful. I'll never forget the first time it hit me hard. I was in Year 8, sitting in English class, when another student shouted out and called me an "Abo" in front of everyone. I was stunned. It cut deep. I remember my teacher Mr. Pope taking me out of class to check if I was okay. The truth was, I wasn't. I felt humiliated, small, and like I didn't belong. The school never gave any repercussions to the racist kid for the incident, and they didn't supply me with any tools or support on how to deal with it.

There are so many different stories. I can talk about the time I experienced racism and discrimination on the footy field when a guy placed my head into the ground after a tackle, called me a Nigger and ran off. Or when a few kids in the crowd started calling me a Nigger when I played one of my first South Australian National Football League (SANFL) footy trial games.

Or the countless times I've walked into a shop, only to have the security guard follow me down every aisle, watching me constantly as if I was going to steal something. Or when work colleagues and myself jumped into a taxi in Brisbane, the taxi man then noticed I was Aboriginal and said he couldn't take us any further. Or when me and my brother were with my uncle crossing the road in Adelaide on our way to a baseball game and some guys driving past called us Niggers. Or when I was in Adelaide walking down my street and police aggressively pulled up on me in their car, asking for my ID and where I was headed. Or when I was driving a flash hire car in Cairns in 2023, and a police officer pulled me over for no reason and asked for my ID to check if I was a criminal. Of course it came back clean, and he let me go. Or when I was walking past Southern Cross Station in Melbourne in 2024 and police stopped me in public as part of their "random checks." They asked for my ID, searched my bag, and patted me down. As I looked around, I only saw other brown people being searched, while the white people were allowed to just continue to walk by, with their white privilege. These are just some of my experiences of racism and racial profiling.

I try to travel as much as I can outside of Australia to escape this treatment, to find more peace away from stereotyping and judgement because of the colour of my skin and my facial features. But in saying that, I do dread coming back and going through customs, as many times I've been racially profiled and checked, again only to see white people just walking by without a worry because of their white privilege. I've tired ways to avoid this, such as by dressing well, but to the racist eye I guess there's no escape. One of the reasons I moved from Adelaide to Melbourne (Naarm) in 2022 was to escape the ongoing racism I experienced, including the casual racism that often goes unnoticed by others. But it is all too familiar to many of us Aboriginal people because we have dealt with it for our whole lives. I thought by moving away from this dark cloud, to a larger multicultural city, that I could maybe blend in more and not be stereotyped. But I quickly learned that racism still finds me here in Naarm. It follows me, no matter where I go in this country. For clarity on what casual racism is, there is a video on YouTube called 'The Invisible Discriminator' created by Beyond Blue.

I remember having a conversation during a recent work photography shoot with a young Aboriginal man with similar skin complexion as mine. In between taking photos, we had an open conversation about racism. He shared also with a colleague, who is white, that he experiences racism all the time, it came as a real shock to her. I also recall a work conference I attended in 2024 targeted at nurses and midwifes who are Aboriginal or Torres Strait Islander. In one session about racism, the facilitator asked everyone to raise their hands if they openly identified as Aboriginal or Torres Strait Islander in their workplace. Nobody raised their hand. It was a telling moment. Some people shared that they choose not to identify to avoid racism, because there was a lack of cultural safety, and no proper systems in place to report it.

In 2024, my workplace held a targeted workforce education session for Aboriginal people working on the frontline in health services. During the session, I was surprised to discover that one of the participants named Jeff was my uncle. We started talking about my Uncle Allan, which led to a well-known story about him. The story goes like this. Uncle Allan was playing in a footy match in a small country town called Whyalla, where I was born and raised. He was playing full forward, waiting for the ball to come down, when he heard a man on the sidelines yelling these racial slurs at him "Nigger", "Abo", and "Boong". Without hesitation, he jumped the fence, ran over, and knocked the racist man out. Then jumped back onto the field just in time to take a great mark and kick a great goal. My uncle Jeff was at that game and saw the whole thing happen and said the crowd went wild with joyful cheers after he did that. Later in the training session, uncle Jeff shared some of his own experiences with racism. One story was about lining up first at a café, only to be ignored while others around him were served. He spoke honestly about how angry and uncomfortable it made him feel. Us mob know very well that this is "casual racism". I could only listen, relate and empathise.

As I get close to finishing writing this book, I'm reminded of something that happened just the other week. I was lining up at a café in St Kilda. I ordered and paid for my coffee, then waited patiently. Ten minutes went by, and I watched as others who had ordered after me received their coffees, one by one. Mine was nowhere to be seen. I knew what was going on. Eventually, once they realised I was still waiting, they asked again what I ordered, then I had to wait a bit longer until they handed over my coffee with an apology for the delay. I took the coffee and just walked past the front counter, giving a silent but frustrated look. Normally, I'd speak up, but these days, I just don't have the energy. Dealing with these ongoing scenarios is really exhausting. And the coffee? It tasted terrible.

In my past 25 years of professional working life, one key aspects across all my roles have been to build genuine rapport with many different Aboriginal Nations in many different communities. This process involved first listening to truth-telling, hearing the gaps and concerns and then over time trying to figure out how best to use each other's strengths and work together to support what they needed. During a visit to a regional town, we met with Aboriginal members of the local workforce. While discussing access to health services, one worker spoke about the ongoing issue of racism, which they said had worsened since the Voice to Parliament. They described open acts of racism and discrimination, such as Aboriginal people being denied service when presenting prescriptions at pharmacies. Another woman shared how she feels unsafe walking through the shops and often deliberately removes her work uniform, which carries Aboriginal branding, to avoid being targeted. Here we are in August 2025, it is still happening today, and as I know from experience that racism is often worse in smaller country towns. Listening to their story was disappointing but not a surprise. I couldn't imagine living in such a small country town and having to face this daily. It was clear that racism had taken a toll on each person but somehow, they still show up every day, do their jobs and try to live their lives the best way they can in this uncomfortable environment. Coming back from my beautiful Bali holiday in September 2025 and hearing about the far-right attack on Camp Sovereignty that happened the same day I landed back in Narrm, it made me want to get back on a flight, and out of this country. I mean, I don't know how we are still here in 2025, with Neo-Nazi figures of a variety of ages, showing up in in broad daylight and physically assaulting numerous Aboriginal people men and women for no reason.

We know that the most important thing in any human's life is health, and everyone should be able to access it safely, regardless of skin colour or race. Yet for many Aboriginal people, health services and hospital settings remain unsafe. In my role, I advocate for change by raising awareness of these issues and advising on ways to end racism and discrimination in health settings.

This work begins with education, implementation of cultural safety and anti-racism education. It's a challenging area of work, where one can easily get burnt out or leave roles due to bureaucratic systems. That's why we need strong alliances between Aboriginal and non-Aboriginal organisations who are genuine allies, combining our strengths to work together to combat the issue of racism. I guess time will tell what kind of culturally safe future we can create for the generations to come.

I can't help but reflect that this journey would be a lot easier if the Voice to Parliament had been voted in, as it would have brought in greater resources and place Aboriginal people at the forefront. In my eyes, it was going to be a way for Aboriginal people to be in the position to advise directly to the highest level of government on priority areas to closing the gap across many different areas. It was a chance to have truth-telling, and recognise the historical facts, like intergenerational trauma, stolen children, genocides, and so on, that have affected Aboriginal people since colonisation. I believe this would have been a good starting point, influencing the long road ahead, to see positive changes, as we know things never happen overnight especially if it's political.

Through this book, I'm asking you to step into my shoes. To pause and reflect. What if any of these situations happened to you or a loved one? How would it make you feel? I ask these tough questions not to shame, but to build empathy, to help others care about something that's still hurting so many people today.

Racism isn't a thing of the past, it's something that still follows many of us like a shadow we never asked for. That's why you all have a responsibility to stand up and challenge it, not just with words, but with actions. To help build a fairer, more compassionate world where no one has to feel that kind of pain.

As a father now, this weighs on me even more. I don't want my daughter to go through the same struggles I did. I speak about this in my song titled "Daughter", under my artist name Col Darcy. It's a reflection of the reality that one day, I'll need to teach her how to navigate racism in this country. Sadly, the Voice to Parliament debate showed us just how present racism still is in Australia. It reminded a lot of us that the fight against it still isn't over. That's why this book exists. To every person reading this, your voice matters. Speak up for what's right. Listen deeply. Be courageous and call out racism and discrimination whenever you see it. Don't stay silent.

And to those with white privilege, understand the power you hold and how you can use it to help dismantle the systems that uphold racism. This burden should not fall on Aboriginal people, we did not create racism and these racist systems, and it should not be our responsibility to change them. Although in saying that, in my professional work life, one aspect of my line of work is I educate about racism. Every time I play videos that show what racism looks like, it triggers me. It brings back painful memories and takes me straight back to the traumatic moments I've lived through. It's incredibly uncomfortable for me, but I do it because if I don't show the reality and the impact, then who will?

That's why we need your help. You all have a shared responsibility to carry this work forward, to speak up, to listen, and to take meaningful action. In Melbourne, there's public spaces like on trams that often feature clear messaging about sexual harassment and antisocial behaviour, along with support lines to report incidents. This approach fosters a culture of accountability and safety. Racism, however, deserves the same level of visibility and seriousness.

We need anti-racism messaging embedded in public spaces across the entire country, not just a few cities, backed by endless resources to keep them ongoing. In Sydney, there are numerous signs posted across the city saying, "Racism Not Welcome". Imagine that across the whole country on public transport, including on aeroplanes, in cafes, restaurants, hospitals, gyms, shopping centres, bars, clubs, workplaces and so on. This kind of visible, proactive approach to combating racism is exactly what I had hoped would be proposed and implemented through the Voice to Parliament, had it been voted in. It must also include dedicated reporting systems or support lines, like those used for sexual harassment, so that people can safely and confidently report racist behaviour as it occurs. City councils, state and federal governments have the power to lead this change. Other relevant businesses can also advocate for it. However, any action must be taken in genuine collaboration and co-design with key members of the local

Aboriginal community in the areas where you operate. Looking at technology and AI, perhaps in the future there could be vocal detection in public spaces that identifies harmful and racist language, such as slurs including Nigger, Boong, Coon, and Abo. This kind of technology could not only hold people accountable but also provide proof when incidents of racism occur. We need strong allyship. This could involve non-Aboriginal people working within Aboriginal-owned education businesses, such as Weenthunga, to actively educate others about racism. This could include leading the delivery of education on what racism is, its impacts, and concepts such as white privilege, white fragility, white anxiety, to help unpack, confront and, dismantle these systems. I still remember seeing Beyond Blue's powerful ad on TV for the first time showing what racism and casual racism is. It struck a major chord with me. As mentioned before, to find it, search "The Invisible Discriminator" on YouTube. I highly recommend this video be watched over and over until the message sinks in and you see what racism and casual racism is and its impacts.

Commercial TV should adopt this resource and replay the campaign during prime time, as well as on major platforms such as AFL football stadiums. As we see, racism is still an issue in this sport, and the AFL can play a major role in bringing this to the forefront. If done, fear for exposing the truth will be broken down, and others will adopt the approach over time because a popular platform set the predicant. At least in my mind, I predict this approach will provide a positive ripple effect and a clear starting point to educate people on the issue. It needs to start with showing people exactly what discrimination, racism and casual racism looks like so they can identify it when it happens and call it out.

At a 2024 Reconciliation conference, I listened to an Aboriginal woman from an AFL Football Club speak on a panel. She spoke about trying to get support from other AFL clubs to stand with them in creating an antiracism campaign. She explained how no other clubs would buy into it. If I was in her position of influence, I would have not given up and strategized to approach other sports such as the NBL and Tennis Australia to seek buy in. But you get the picture, there is a want and need for change within mainstream platforms, steered by Aboriginal people in identified roles. Hopefully over time we will see anti racism campaigns implemented across many commercial platforms.

I recently visited Adelaide and took part in an art workshop at an Aboriginal cultural centre. With my daughter on my lap, painting a boomerang, us mob started yarning in a truth-telling way and we spoke about many different issues, one being about the justice system. Unfortunately, deaths in custody of Aboriginal people have been and is still a big issue in this country. Officers in prison systems are harming and even killing Aboriginal people and getting away with it with no repercussions. One of the Elders, a prominent member of South Australia's Aboriginal community, shared his story about dealing with a recent situation of the unfair treatment of an Aboriginal man in prison. As he spoke, he explained how this Aboriginal man was placed into solitary confinement for close to 800 days, instead of the regulated 15 days maximum. This well-respected leader shared that he wasn't allowed to visit the Aboriginal man in prison to offer his support to help resolve the issue, apparently because the prison found out that he had spoken to "The Voice". For those who don't know what The Voice is, it's basically the South Australian equivalent of a Victorian Treaty. I strongly advise you to research them both to get more clarity on their individual ways of functioning, vision and purpose. As we listened more to this leader vent about how he was denied visitation to make a change to an unfair situation, I could only listen and feel a sense of hopelessness inside. Because as well as himself being denied access to help, a support worker inside the prison who was Aboriginal, was also denied access to do her job and help. Not long after, she was forced out of her position, the very kind of workforce support our mob need in place to stop unfair treatment and harm, gone... This is why Aboriginal people continue to march and protest the racist systems and the injustices that we still face today.

Justice is truly served when policies, laws, and systems actively protect Aboriginal people from harm, and when those who break these laws are held accountable. It is served when both past and present wrongs against Aboriginal people are acknowledged, and when policy change is embraced through platforms such as the Victorian Treaty. It's amazing to now see a Victorian Treaty introduced into parliament to reckon with past wrongs and empower Victoria's First Peoples. In prison systems, there needs to be a thorough vetting and appointment process to ensure the right workforce is selected, ensuring people will do more good than harm, with leaders at every level setting the standard by acting with integrity and doing what is right.

Recently I attended an event in Melbourne, "Speaking Truth to Power", hosted by the Yoorrook Justice Commission, where I heard powerful stories of truth-telling. One story that stayed with me was about a young girl experiencing racism at school. A parent noticed their child coming home one day and scrubbing her skin. At first, they didn't understand why. The little girl eventually explained that other kids at school were bullying her because of her skin colour. She was trying to make her skin white so she wouldn't be targeted. I also recently heard from a senior stakeholder in the Department of Education that many children, who are Aboriginal, are still reporting experiences of racism at school. It was also mentioned during this meeting that schools across the state didn't have enough resources in yearly budgets to provide anti-racism education to combat this. It deeply concerns me that our young mob are facing these harsh realities, that children are made to feel anxious, ashamed of their identity, and that having darker skin somehow makes them less. No child should have to carry that burden.

Repercussions need to be given out to those inflicting these wrongs. It is when those who perpetuate racism are held to account, and when society unites to challenge and eliminate racism in all its forms. Change begins when individuals take the time to understand what racism is, recognise its impact, grow empathy through that process, and care enough to take meaningful, proactive steps to end it.

By making it this far, you should now have a clear understanding of what racism looks like and gained meaningful insights into its impact. This is a resource that can be used across a range of settings, from communities and workplaces to schools and universities. Now that you've read, reflected, and written your responses, the responsibility is yours, speak up, share what you've learned, and actively educate others, whether that's your friends, family, colleagues, or community members.

Together, we can create a future where no one ever has to ask:

"HOW WOULD YOU LIKE TO BE ME?"